THE WILSON POEMS

ALSO BY IAN RANDALL WILSON

Poetry
Theme of the Parabola (a chapbook)

Fiction
Absolute Knowledge: Stories
Great Things Are Coming (a novella)
Hunger and Other Stories
Out of the Arcadian Ghetto (a fiction chapbook)

THE WILSON POEMS

A Chapbook

Ian Randall Wilson

Hollyridge Press
Venice, California

© 2009 Ian Randall Wilson

All rights reserved under International and Pan-American Copyright Conventions. Published in the United States by Hollyridge Press.

Hollyridge Press
P.O. Box 2872
Venice, California 90294
www.hollyridgepress.com

Cover Design by Rio Smyth
Author Photo by Richard P. Gabriel
Manufactured in the United States of America by Lightning Source

ISBN-13: 978-0-9799588-6-1
ISBN-10: 0-9799588-6-5

Grateful acknowledgment is made to the editors of the following publications where these poems first appeared:

Both Magazine: "World View"
Descant: "The Better Stone"; "The Clinic"
Mudlark: "The Expectation of Wilson"; "The Hollywood Meditations"; "Wilson Abandons His Muses"; "Wilson Discourses on the Personal"; "Wilson Exercises His Classical Education"; "Wilson, Cleared"; "Wilson's First Film Set"
Spork: "Wilson On a Deserted Island"; "Wilson, As Everyone Does in Hollywood, Has a Second Career"; "Wilson, Produces"; "Wilson's Annual Check-Up"
Tin Luster Mobile: "My Other Faces"

Contents

Wilson Exercises His Classical Education	3
Wilson Discourses on the Personal	6
Wilson Abandons His Muses	8
Wilson's First Film Set	10
The Hollywood Meditations	12
The Expectation of Wilson	14
Wilson, as Does Everyone in Hollywood, Has a Second Career	16
Wilson, Produces	17
Wilson's Annual Check-Up	19
Wilson on a Deserted Island	21
World View	24
Wilson, Cleared	25
My Other Faces	26
Wilson and the Swan, While Leda Watches	28
First Called (A Ghazal)	29
A State Passing (A Ghazal)	30
Known Equations (A Ghazal)	31
The Clinic (A Ghazal)	32
The Better Stone (A Ghazal)	33
Last Call (A Ghazal)	34

The Wilson Poems

WILSON EXERCISES HIS CLASSICAL EDUCATION

"The spit-camel of the Sahara
doesn't have to drink for a month."
I learn this on the Discovery Channel.
I, on the other hand, find myself pissing each hour.
This makes for difficult sleep.
So it's pasta again tonight,
sauce from a jar.
I dream I have the heart of a lion in the body of a trout,
this makes for a cat who can breathe underwater.
I have no time to process this image
because my dog is demanding
to be fed.
My culinary skills have not progressed beyond
flicking the burner on.
My burners are sealed.
They develop 40,000 BTU's.
That's power, baby, this stainless steel
commercial grade Viking range
sits quiet most nights.
I don't lament her leaving
and taking the cats.
She chose between a supporting role
in the new Madonna vehicle and staying home—
what would you have done?

When I was young I walked to the movies
and got lost in the dark.
Tonight I don't bother.
I depend upon desert.
I pass a cheesecake and my heart throbs.

I pass two women discussing cheesecake
and I follow them home.
A company films outside my favorite restaurant
and I can't get to the door.
Shoe, shouts a man holding a stick, *Betty, Five K.*
These are the codes of a street obstructed by silver trucks,
the sidewalks blackened by power cords.
I try to step lightly between fixtures
when I fall into the shot.
It's the fault of my big feet that
I get discovered, the director rushes to my side,
all this happening to a man who hates cameras and persists
in sitting at the back of every room.

When the police finish questioning me
about why I disrupted the shoot,
I go back to my house and clip all the hairs from my nose.
I can breathe easier now
and work on my ears.
This thrill of aging
sends me to the couch.
Stronger glasses, bigger pants,
these are the reasons she left me
and that I'm on a first-name basis with Vool,
the delivery man from Domino's on Ocean Park.
Discarded pizza boxes make excellent insulation.
I heard this on television.
Save the planet
build a house
from pizza boxes and newspapers
and oriented strand board culled from waste growth trees.

When I turn on the television, the plant on top
begins to grow. In the time it takes to water it,
she is there, selling cars.
Expensive cars.
Vool will be here in ten minutes.
I hope he can fix the color;
she looks a bit red.

WILSON DISCOURSES ON THE PERSONAL

Finally the personal
is all I can hold onto,
the vanishing sill between foundation and wall.
What is authenticity to a frog?
I have spent years inventing
my parents—divorcing them, killing them off
in piece after piece.
Never allowing them to come together,
I negate my existence through their disunion.
I pit fictitious brothers against themselves,
make sisters hate.
Then I set myself up as an only child,
emperor of the toy box, the one pony.
What can be more personal than a list of lovers
who have passed from the scene?
The name of everyone I ever lied to
beginning and ending with me?

A man walks into a house, the door closes, and he is alone.
From other rooms a wife appears, children, even cats.
Time passes and he is again alone, gravitating
toward his natural state. For a moment
I don't doubt the sadness
but because I say it doesn't make it true—
only ducks are that sincere.

In the instant I believe I have grasped
all the possible permutations of a life,
something new presents itself,
a thing that might startle,
perhaps incest this time
might confirm to myself there is being, not emptiness,
a man remotely resembling a man that is me.

WILSON ABANDONS HIS MUSES

The beagle showed me the way to my first great poem.
All that white hair, the long long snout,
I never saw it before
the start of my many publications,
and then I understood the unmistakable
facial similarity to Robert Frost.

Success continued until one day the cat urged me
in a different direction: all swagger
and mince and murderous whim. Frank O'Hara.
I should have known
from those perky little ears,
that, and the rolling drunkard's gait.

Of course the dog and the cat didn't get along.
Discordant aesthetics brought tension
to my home, so I have taken
to writing outside.
A bird who could pass for Rimbaud
has accosted me. *The blue nut grows houses*,
cries a squirrel in the voice of Breton.

I need to go some place sterile,
where the birds and the bees and the plants can't get to me,
a sealed room with filtered air and filtered light
where I won't be subject to influences.

Then and only then can I claim the words on the page.
If the walls don't start talking,
if the floor stays quiet,
if the ceiling doesn't render an opinion
on the quality of my verse.

WILSON'S FIRST FILM SET

A man rushes into a paint store and shouts:
I need to paint a banana.
Where's the yellow?

Now in your town, if a man rushes into a paint store and announces he is painting bananas I'm willing to bet that the clerk would roll his eyes, make that circular movement with an index finger round the temple, suggest you find the door.
At Standard Brands in Hollywood, clerks rush to your aid, knowing it must be some movie, believing that they, too, are part of immortality.
So I am holding a banana
standing in a paint store
in Hollywood
examining bottles of paint.
For twenty minutes we compare paint samples,
decide on something water-based,
quick drying,
easily applied by hand.
We test different types on the banana to cover all its flaws—eventually producing a peerless fruit: ripe, necessary, totally made up.
With extra bottles of paint, brushes, thinner and other solvents for cleaning, I return to the set.

The commercial actors are striking and it's up to us to get the product shot,
meaning that as a production assistant charged with carrying boxes, getting food for the director, delivering cans of film, I am part of one vast enterprise of filmmakers, of artists who daily sell you bread.
After ten hours with a tray of tomatoes
the director isn't satisfied.
They're not red enough, he decides, we need to make them weep, glisten with sexual abundance.
He says, I want tomatoes you can screw.
In this Hollywood, no one sees
that I have gone to film school
—prestigious film school, I might add—
spent years working on my craft.
I know more about lighting, cameras, film than surgeons know about hearts.
Get ready with the bananas, the assistant tells me,
we might have to go to them quick.
This is how we sell produce when the actors are on strike and a parrot stands in for the usual spokesman for the grocery store chain, a soap opera star.
So I am here with the bananas for the next insert,
lining up the boxes, ready with my paint.
Meanwhile we finish the tomatoes,
will go to lettuce after lunch
while the leaves maintain some green
before they wilt.
I think about filters.
The actor prepares.
How I'd frame the shot.
How I'd bring out the emotion in the fruit,
acting naturally,
to find and lose all sense of self.

THE HOLLYWOOD MEDITATIONS

During the lunch break while the executives dine at LA Farm,
 I jerk off in front of the Mitsubishi.
Enough ambition for today, lost in a cloth.
The skin offers a fine resistance
for ten seconds.
I have traded away the real thing by sending off the Beloved
 for the afternoon taking cats to the holistic vet for
 their shot of herbs.
Later they will meditate.
I understand the mind of God
becomes visible during sex.
I am watching Misty Blue part her knees while Jerry North
 heads south, moving in among those meatless bruised
 happy thighs for the close-up.
And I am all used up. Hollywood, some call it.
On the stairs outside a small office in the Valley, miles
 from Hollywood and Vine, which is itself miles from
 that Hollywood appearing on your screen, on the stairs
 the men are waiting.
Their line goes into the street where it is Wednesday.
Watch ambition.
The police allow this weekly ritual, they leave the line
 alone.
Here, the only thing that matters is the size of the cock:
 size means length, thickness, circumference.
Boldness in the Trade.
Misty Blue arrives and nods her head choosing three hopefuls
 to once more mark her thighs.

At work I sit in a screening room and watch poor framing,
    another error by the projectionist; at $22.50 an hour,
    he doesn't have a care.
We let our best man go to Sony.
Now we have to rent him back.
The optical track is wavering by the side of the screen like
    snakes running up a wall.
Not my metaphor.
I have borrowed it from the sound man and I ask him: Does
    he want it back?
Five men in suits walk down the corridor all holding phones;
    some say power drifts behind them.
They need to make us laugh to keep their jobs.
I have no trouble laughing, I start on Monday and by the
    middle of the week I grow exhausted by all the mirth.
After that I close my door and worry.
Will my talent never ripen?

THE EXPECTATION OF WILSON

I'm the one who ends up in the kitchen
doling out the beers
and the women who stay for any length of time
are looking for a man in another line of work.
I spend my days around lawyers.
Last year they wrote a thousand contracts
that I put in their proper files
ready for immediate retrieval.
Our filing system is impressive
though I can't tell you what we do.
Of course I can tell you
but I don't have the full knowledge to explain it myself.
It's something about foreign television rights,
bad pilots that never aired.
"Baywatch" is high art compared to what we sell—
but that has nothing to do with me,
wandering into an office each morning at nine.
Without an inner life to speak of, I drink my coffee.
I answer the phone and, most important, I have mastered
the art of the paper cut.
I staple and type, and change
the bottled water by the clock.
I believed I would grow up to be powerful, known,
but after listening to twelve continuous hours of motivational
      tapes,
I have become the kind of man who punches holes in walls,
opening a space between the nothing that is not there
on Tuesdays and the nothing that is nothing.

I lament my lack of journal entries
from the beginning of my youth.

I can't remember my childhood.
My father, in his dementia, burned all the pictures,
took the house with him in his funeral pyre.
My boss is concerned.
He believes that his people shouldn't wear black eyes,
cross their knuckles in scabs that ooze.
I have to agree.
The laundry has been calling.
The blood-stains are impossible to remove
from my white cotton shirts.
There's nothing we can do, they tell me,
nothing to do,
and there's that nothing that is
again, coming at me from another source.

WILSON, AS DOES EVERYONE IN HOLLYWOOD, HAS A SECOND CAREER

Like Hogan with his golf, he is always *practicing*.
Sometimes he practices so hard his hands bleed which makes
      for messy keyboards, computer failure.
This year he has bought two new machines
and taken to wearing latex
in the hours of his writing.
With this effective waterproof barrier
his words come more easily.
Interviewed by his company's in-house news organ, Wilson
      tells them there is not enough daylight in a day to
      practice all the words you ought to be practicing.
Thank God for electric light, the editor says.

WILSON, PRODUCES

I wake up in the wrong womb:
cat vomit or perhaps it is my own.
This movement backward,
what misplaced exaltation—
and too much champagne at Chaya Venice with an ingenue
    half my age.
When I was half my age, a taxi brought me to a film premier
    where paparazzi rushed the door. In the white light
    of all their strobing, I believed I saw the face of
    God.
Then someone shouted, *He's no one.*
Now I feed the cats and wait until it's light.
While my tea is steeping I rake the litter box restoring
    symmetry in the sweeping of my tool, I would add rocks
    and a few perennials but the cats disdain the
    decoration: they want to pose in peace.

This is sad.
The Beloved is an actress shooting out of town.
The Beloved was once an ingenue.
Our faces melt with age and though I hide mine under a
    beard hers must go bare.
How does an actress name herself, take off her clothes so
    the head shot features skin?
Now producers look past her when she walks into a room,
    cameras point their lenses elsewhere.

When the Beloved returns
she will signal, edging closer to the bedroom door.
Although she doesn't want them, I hope to give her sons.
I decide to call in sick,
decide to lie back down.
Tomorrow, when the Beloved returns, we will eat vegetables
      grown by the deaf and hand out money to the homeless,
      we will give up meat and drink holy water purchased at
      the store, take our fruits organic, then have to beg
for bread.
Hallelujah.

WILSON'S ANNUAL CHECK-UP

I have flounder tonight,
think trout tomorrow,
tuna on the weekend.
It was fish that sent me to my parents, overhearing
 conversations about the true nature of love.
Still I wanted to fall in love,
love, love, love, love, love, love, love, love, until the
 word stopped making sense.
Instead I fell down the stairs.
Tripped, I'm sure.
Years later I learn the pains are much the same.
I have a tendency to stumble
while talking to a woman.
Every long bone has been broken twice.
Their words make me tingle.
I saved all the casts.
On rainy days my ribs grow hot and I suppress the urge to
 rip them from my chest.
Cher had her floating rib removed as did Bo Derek.
This is why I avoid Seattle and flee to drier climates at
 the first forecasts of rain.
Strangely, I am unaffected by snow although in the higher
 elevations my interior tissues swell and I am prone to
 an endless bleeding of the nose.

I have lived at sea level all my life within sight of the
 ocean.
Safety in the swells.

I can't imagine life under a bridge with all my world's
 possessions tied up in a sack.
Once I pretended I ended up in North Carolina in a monk's
 cloister learning how to write.
The woods encroached and there was too much nature.
My feet hung over the bed,
and that gruel they served us daily began to green.
Surely there is a story here, though
this is not the necessary.
Beyond the scattered words I offer throughout the day at
 work, I am alone for hours with the door closed
 breathing artificial air.
I am earning. Something.
Once I imagined myself a hockey goalie
unable to find the net,
a fisherman without hooks who calls out to his fish.
How Zen are we this morning?
When I die, I want no trace of me to linger.
Cross out all references to my name.
I want my body burned and then my ashes burned again.
Immolate my papers.

WILSON ON A DESERTED ISLAND

     1.
Disco reasserts itself
though the rains are expected
and an actor's strike before next month.
Nineteen nights last month I went out dancing, drank
     Smirnoff's cold, grappled with strangers half my age
     and half the ones I told about my business willfully
     made my bed.
I said I was a director and in the noise
of the club my title escaped them.
In fact, I put family photos on film
and spend the rest of my time in middle management.
I may be out of work.

     2.
Without the lights on, at what angles do bodies collide?
In this equation, when a train leaves Chicago on Wednesday
     at 3:24 heading due South and another train leaves
     Topeka the day before will they ever meet?
I have forgotten to factor in the speeds.
Don't worry—I was protected.

     3.
This morning another natural disaster of suspicious origin:
     no milk.
Yesterday, a breakdown in juice communication.
I believe we are holding out from going to the store.
Without paper products or soap, things could get edgy
     around here.

    4.
When I met her she was an actress on a cable access show and I was the second grip. I had to stay out of her way.
She looked lovely with a scrim shading her face.
But now on the sudden morning of January, when we fear the presence of El Niño and are sure we're going to drown, she is groggy and the backs of her arms are sagging.

    5.
I have forgotten the taboo of intercourse with strangers, on eating and drinking, on showing the face, on quitting the house, on leaving food over.
Iron is taboo. Blood is taboo. Sharp weapons are taboo. Spittle is taboo. Knots and rings are taboo.
To speak the name of any god is to invite the failure of crops.
At my company we do not mention the chairman
except as Himself.

    6.
Remodeling doesn't change
the color of my rugs.
Dust flies
when the Beloved slams the door.

7.
Last month I stopped going out.
This month I unplug the phone,
end my newspaper subscriptions
toss all magazines into the trash, unread.
I cut the phone cord and break the television's screen.
Now at work to get past language,
I trip the breakers, still the radio, turn out the lights.
At last, isolation. From outside, I appear to be a man
       lost in thought.

WORLD VIEW

The thing I like about cold apples
is how the flesh snaps
when I eat to the core.
In the alley out back
two brothers begin to argue.
I assume they're brothers
because of the matching hands.
If the violence of their words were spume,
the whole road would be under water.
As it is we are happy
there aren't any knives.
Pear?
A truck and the jacaranda
grow another inch.
You know that's it for breakfast.
What part of any day is good?
A teacher many years ago
predicted this outcome:
Come away from the window, Mr. Wilson,
it's no good watching the world—
and here I am again.
I can see 20 feet
in two directions
and anyone walking beyond my sliver of view
creeps into someone's else's universe.
The bones of my neck crack
announcing the start
of another race.
Someone is shouting back there.

WILSON, CLEARED

Sometimes a closing door
stands in for love's first stages,
imminence in the smack of bodies,
the way the parts all fit together
and then they don't.
It was me she waited for,
to say I'm sorry, on a winter afternoon
between semesters when she caught me with someone else.
I've never been good at denial,
and who can be when discovered red-handed, red-faced,
between the open legs of the stolen goods?

Sometimes a closing door
advances toward its frame
holding daylight on one side
to let new lovers start.
I can't apologize for lacking finite answers,
and the one I slept with years ago—
it only happened once, once.
All this talk of doors in metal
sandwiched between wood,
hollow-cored and insulated,
glass low-boys and the ones that come in red,
weather-stripping refurbished,
the insulation factor nearing ten—
the metaphor can't change the facts:
She went out the front and kept on walking.
I climbed back into bed.

MY OTHER FACES

Ian Wilson is trying to walk
Ian Wilson is a composer of imaginative resource and a sure
 formal sense
Ian Wilson is a very nice guy
Ian Wilson is confident about his next
Ian Wilson is one of the strongest voices in the younger
 generation of irish composers
Ian Wilson is a leading expert on
Ian Wilson is the final product of a four part series
Ian Wilson is prepared to pass the hat around local businesses
Ian Wilson is the
Ian Wilson is a member of the british columbia association of
 professional consulting archaeologists
Ian Wilson is very optimistic about the lenders acquisition
Ian Wilson is considered to be the foremost shroud authority
Ian Wilson is hoping to see tangible progress on the $166
Ian Wilson is a post
Ian Wilson is to organise the finer details
Ian Wilson is son
Ian Wilson is a fantasy & sci
Ian Wilson is currently holding 10th place but that will
 definitely not last
Ian Wilson is just outside the top ten in the "wee opel" despite
 a broken disc caliper
Ian Wilson is still convinced that the shroud of turin contained
 the body of christ
Ian Wilson is visiting the people in daresbury
Ian Wilson is a physics
Ian Wilson is gevraagd een discussie te leiden
Ian Wilson is a historian
Ian Wilson is a well balanced review of the misty facts

Ian Wilson is another favorite writer on religious topics
Ian Wilson is leaving for nigeria where he will be part of an evangelistic team
Ian Wilson is a retired fishing boat skipper
Ian Wilson is listed at cumbernauld
Ian Wilson is
Ian Wilson is the possibility of freshening the midfield
Ian Wilson is supportive of all efforts
Ian Wilson is the following link
Ian Wilson is waiting for a hand injury
Ian Wilson is now <iwilson@salecollege>
Ian Wilson is supervising the work
Ian Wilson is an authority on the issue of artistic tradition
Ian Wilson is the composer
Ian Wilson is also very good at avoiding discussion of the polonius/burghley connection
Ian Wilson is a bit too flattering
Ian Wilson is

WILSON AND THE SWAN, WHILE LEDA WATCHES

A sudden change in the angle of the sun
reflecting off sheer stones beside them
and the great bird misses his intended.
Suddenly it is Wilson
grabbed up and shadowed
under the spread of wings.
He is held
fast by the bill
a caress among brothers.
But there is intention
there in the thrusting loins,
the shudder and release
wasted, all those generations
that will not be engendered.
Surely he must know as he flies off,
must understand that without Leda
Troy will not follow
or the flowering of Greece.
Enter Leda, now at Wilson's side.
She spends the afternoon removing down
from his hair and repaying him
the only way she knows how.

FIRST CALLED (A Ghazal)

He traces back his name to the time it was first imagined, then given, then spoken aloud the sounds dissipating into a world.
He speaks now, and nothing changes.
It is difficult learning a substitute for love.
He leaves that to those who know the word for the man first called upon to interpret the falling of snow
When crops failed.
In another language flowers drawn against blue represents divinity.
In French it is *fleur*.
Four dozen roses and still she must leave.
This comes from inventing other gods in place of the one true.
She called at the height of the raining season when ceremonies were required to keep the waters down by his door.
She announces a change, allowed she would go so far as to begin to like shrubs.
He spoke her name, called out his own to confirm a self as you might, Ian, shaken from the depths of the last sleep to discover words have no sources, nothing grown bears weight.

A STATE PASSING (A Ghazal)

The verb form is simplest in its present tense.
He will go. He is going.
He is gone
He goes to the cherished reward.
Age is that adjective which begins to modify confusion.
Though we still believe we understand the future or at least perceive its general shape.
"Please do not resuscitate me," he begs. "Don't let them tie me off"
As if to say that medicine has failed him in the abstract but the doctors can still manufacture a state passing for a life.
What can we do for our lover when his spirit asks release in the light of God teachings which refuse to honor the form in its present tense?
How do I kill you? Let me count the ways.
He went
With a measure of the peaceful after the bag descended on his head as you hope you will, Ian, without the need for anyone by the bed.

KNOWN EQUATIONS (A Ghazal)

The props vary only in the color of the sheets, the queen or
    king or double-sized spread.
To make love on such a surface is an act of violence for those
    who do not feel.
Ancient Persian scholars discovered four hundred separate nerve
    ends within the mushroomed head.
Many died to give that number shape.
There is a man leaning against the door with his shirt still
    buttoned and he is feeling
Nothing.
The pliancy of box springs is part of known equations.
He cuts his arms for the reaction.
With a high clotting factor the flow is quickly stemmed.
All women bleed longer.
At the height of noon following the equinox a white line re-
    veals itself across his wrist most visible to him when he
    brushes off his eyes, as you do, Ian, before you close
    the door.

THE CLINIC (A Ghazal)

What we have borne between us this afternoon will change.
In the room with five walls only women are allowed.
The corridor branching right marks the world, one sort of
 medicine where white coats and pressed lips imitate
 calm.
According to some life ends under erasure.
Others say, here, mistakes can be corrected.
It is a game of architects.
I hope the refuse is not given to the worms, this still misting
 that might have formed another as me but we have
 reached the age when giving up may be easier though
 desire sets us on.
The silence of clenched teeth loves deeper than any grave.
I am overcome by silence.
Such whisperings with each opening of the beveled door, the
 lack of wailing.
If in law this simple thing is not life, not son, not particle
 known, it is then, Ian, how you define a future waiting
 on a padded table, chrome and straps and the leaching
 of all heat.

THE BETTER STONE (A Ghazal)

The size of a man's headstone is a measure of his lasting
 weight.
Its height, and the depth of the inscription, are markers in the
 league of rank.
In money's consequence, granite makes the better stone.
Marble is the best of all.
This, friends say, matters in a material world.
There is no discussion of the way we die, if the one who goes
 in silence is larger than the one who screams all gods'
 names.
Once a year the book of life is written, the names block
 printed allegedly by some celestial pen.
Belief is not at issue.
Fathers, we hope, vanish before their sons eliminating need for
 shrines.
Still the chosen linger in defiance of their sin.
But at the last, it is those whose sudden changing earns them
 peace as you may, Ian, rocking in your bed waiting on
 a father to call you from this place.

LAST CALL (A Ghazal)

Hell if I'll play longer in this puzzled love for her,
excuse the stones in the dirt that covers her.

After other women turn their backs on me
I'll touch myself and think I glove her.

Witch, beldam, siren, hag—
by now you gather she is no dove her.

I like to make up stories with better endings—
everything that lies I've placed above her.

One night, ten nights, a hundred dark, yes, Ian,
this new gun will stop you thinking of her.